Rebellion in Newark

Random House · *New York*

Tom Hayden

Rebellion
in
Newark

Official Violence and

Ghetto Response

Contents

	Introduction	3
I	*Wednesday: John Smith Starts a Riot*	9
II	*Thursday: The Community Takes Over*	23
III	*The Occupation*	37
IV	*The Terror*	45
V	*From Riot to Revolution?*	63

APPENDIX: *The Dead and Brutalized*   73

                                  The Dead   74

                                  The Killings of Toto and Moran   84

                                  Testimony from the Brutalized   88

Maps appear on pages 11 and 25.

Rebellion in Newark

Introduction

THIS BOOK describes the riot that shook Newark, New Jersey, from July 12 to 17, 1967. More than that, this book seeks to clarify why America is the only affluent Western society where insurrection is a regular happening in its major cities.

White Americans trying to understand without prejudice the violent events of the last four summers will find two themes developed here. The first is that riots are much more than "antisocial behavior." They must be viewed both as a new stage in the development of Negro protest against racism, and as a logical outgrowth of the failure of the whole society to support racial equality. The second theme is that Americans have to turn their attention from the law-breaking violence of the rioters to the original and greater violence of racism, which is supported indirectly by the white community as a whole. Thirty

3

years after the New Deal and five years after the rediscovery of poverty, the question concerned Americans must ask is whether this country is capable, here and now, of dealing with the social problems being violently protested in the slums.

This book is also for people who have actively participated in the civil rights and anti-poverty efforts of the last decade. The riots represent the assertion of new methods of opposing the racism that politics, nonviolence, and community organization have failed to end. This new reality in the ghetto is causing a crisis of strategy, and perhaps of conscience, among those used to acting as spokesmen or organizational representatives of the Negro community. The riot is real; the civil rights activists will have to decide whether it is legitimate and, more important, how to work in relation to it. These issues deserve the fullest possible discussion in the civil rights movement.

The author of these pages is a white man who has spent the past four years in the Newark ghetto organizing around issues of housing, welfare, and political power. During the riot I listened, watched and worked with people. Immediately afterwards I decided the most important task for myself was to suggest to "the outside world" a way of understanding the violence that took place. All of the instances cited in this book are documented by eyewitness accounts or newspaper reports.

Some may wonder whether an objective analysis can be given by one so deeply committed; each reader will have to judge this question for himself, but it is hoped that this record of experiences is honest and clear enough to be used by others who may not share all the conclusions.

* * *

Most of the book is about the five days of crisis, but a few statements about Newark on the eve of the riot may serve as background to the real story.

When Newark exploded, *Life* magazine called it "the predictable insurrection" because conditions in Newark were known to be terrible.

Leaders of the business and political communities knew as much long before the violence broke out. Business officials announced in January 1967 that their own studies showed Newark's problems to be "more grave and pressing than those of perhaps any other American city." Political officials described this grim reality in their spring application for planning funds under the Model Cities Act. According to the application, Newark has the nation's highest percentage of bad housing, the most crime per 100,000 people, the heaviest per capita tax burden, the highest rates of venereal disease, maternal mortality and new cases of tuberculosis. The city is listed second in infant mortality, second in birth rate, seventh in the absolute number of drug addicts. Its unemployment rate, more than 15 per cent in the Negro community, has been persistently high enough to qualify Newark as one of the five cities to get special assistance under the Economic Development Act.

But knowledge of the problems was not enough. Important business and political figures were deadlocked with civil rights groups over the proper solutions. The elites tended to propose pouring money into job training and social service programs through the existing agencies of government. Their priority was to restore Newark as a city suitable for business, commerce, and middle-class residents. The Chamber of Commerce newsletter, *Exec,* called for a new convention arena downtown as part of a development plan to "overwhelm the creeps" currently inhabiting Newark. The summer issue of the Chamber of Commerce magazine promised a "new life in Newark" on its cover. The article within complained that the positive features of Newark, especially its closeness to New York City and its rich undeveloped resources, are overlooked too often because of the "partially true" rumors that Newark is "crowded, it has slums, and *the Negro population is growing rapidly."* The city's vast programs for urban renewal, highways, downtown development, and most recently a 150-acre Medical School, in the heart of the ghetto, seemed almost deliberately designed to squeeze out this rapidly growing Negro community that represents a majority of the population.

Civil rights and anti-poverty activists saw the proper solution in terms of power, rather than money, for the black majority. Black people occupied only token positions in city administrative and political life, and these positions were more dependent on the Mayor's will than the support of ghetto voters. Negro leaders blamed government and social agencies for fostering and neglecting problems, using federal funds to bolster their patronage rolls rather than meeting the crisis of the city. In the weeks before the riot, tensions between the government and the Negro leadership were never greater. Nearly 1000 Negroes disrupted Board of Education meetings when Mayor Hugh Addonizio tried to appoint a Democratic Party ally to an educational post over a fully-qualified Negro candidate. Another large group carried on a filibuster for weeks at Planning Board hearings on the decision to declare "blighted" the site for the Medical School. Addonizio changed his mind only slightly on the education appointment, leaving the post filled by the man who held it before. The Planning Board ended its hearings without yielding to the protest against the Medical School. Many speakers at the hearings, including leaders of the Negro Democratic "establishment," warned that Newark was on the verge of bloodshed and destruction.

Many analysts of the riot will believe that the stage was set by these developments. Newark had not improved; in fact, it had become worse in the eyes of middle-class Negroes who previously had stakes in law and order. The angry outlook of the middle class was spreading into the consciousness of the total black community.

Yet neither city officials nor the civil rights leaders quite believed that a riot was coming. The Chamber of Commerce magazine quoted Addonizio as confidently saying that his "open door" administration had the confidence of Newark Negroes. The only people who wanted violence were a few agitators, the Mayor's side told the *New York Times* in May. Civil rights leaders, too, despite their militant warnings, tended to feel that Newark might remain quiet. After all, Newark was quiet when riots were breaking out in nearby Jersey City and Paterson three years ago. The gossip of many civil rights activists centered on the mysteries of *whether* Newark would explode rather than on what to do *when* Newark did.

I

Wednesday:

John Smith Starts a Riot

As IF to prove its inevitability, the Newark riot began with an ordinary police-brutality incident against a man with an ordinary name: John Smith, driver of Cab 45, in the employ of the Safety Cab Company. Early Wednesday night, Smith's cab drove around a police car double-parked on 15th Avenue. Two uniformed patrolmen stopped the cab. According to the police story given to the *Star-Ledger* of July 14, Smith was charged with "tailgaiting" and driving the wrong way on a one-way street. Later they discovered his license had expired. The officers charged that Smith used abusive language and punched them. "They only used necessary force to subdue Smith, the policemen asserted."

This "necessary force" was described more fully

by Smith at his bail hearing on July 13. "There was no resistance on my part. That was a cover story by the police. They caved in my ribs, busted a hernia, and put a hole in my head." Witnesses on the stoops saw Smith dragged, paralyzed, to the police station. Smith was conscious, however: "After I got into the precinct six or seven other officers along with the two who arrested me kicked and stomped me in the ribs and back. They then took me to a cell and put my head over the toilet bowl. While my head was over the toilet bowl I was struck on the back of the head with a revolver. I was also being cursed while they were beating me. An arresting officer in the cell block said, 'This baby is mine.' "

It was about 8 o'clock. Negro cab-drivers circulated the report on Smith over their radios. Women and men shook their heads as they stood or sat in front of their homes. The word spread down 17th Avenue west of the precinct, and across the avenue into Hayes Homes. Called the "projects" by everyone, Hayes Homes was erected in the wake of "slum clearance" in the mid-Fifties. Each of the six buildings holds about 1000 people on twelve floors. People know them as foul prisons and police know them as "breeding grounds" for crime. As the word spread through Hayes Homes, people gathered at the windows and along the shadowy sidewalks facing the precinct.

What was out of the ordinary about John Smith's case was the fact that the police were forced to let

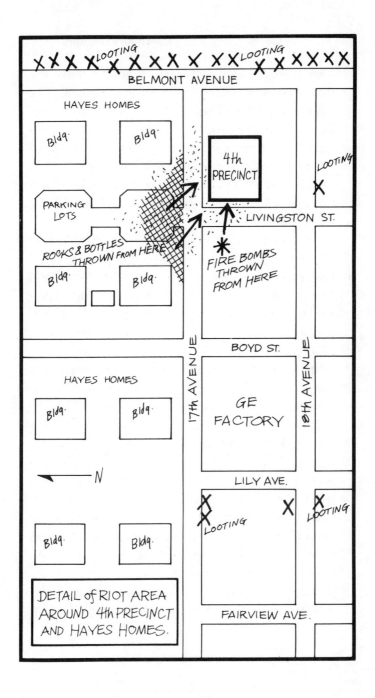

respected civil-rights leaders see his condition less than two hours after the beating happened. The police were trapped and nervous because they were caught by civil-rights leaders who could not be discredited. A neighborhood resident had called several of these leaders—activists from CORE, the United Freedom Party, and the Newark Community Union Project, among others—minutes after Smith was brought in.

After heated argument about Smith with officers in the precinct, an inspector arrived from central police headquarters who let the group see Smith in his cell. "Don't listen to what he says. He's obviously upset and nervous as you might expect," the inspector advised. The group was incensed after seeing Smith's condition, and demanded that he be sent immediately to the hospital. The police complied, and Smith was taken to Beth Israel Hospital. Others searched for witnesses, lawyers, and members of Smith's family.

It was at this point, witnesses who were in the precinct house say, that the police began putting on riot helmets. None of the activists felt there was going to be an explosion, and none remembers a crowd in the street of more than a hundred at this point.

Poverty-program officials, whom the activists had phoned from the precinct, arrived next. Among them were Timothy Still, president of the poverty program, a resident of Hayes Homes and for ten years president of its Tenants' Council, and Oliver Lofton, administrator of the Newark Legal Services Project.

A former assistant U.S. attorney, Lofton would later become the Governor's informal liaison with different elements of the organized Negro community and a member of the Governor's "Blue Ribbon Commission" to investigate the riots. With the knowledge of the police, the leaders determined to organize a peaceful but angry demonstration in front of the precinct. They were given a bullhorn by a police official who hoped they could calm the crowd which was now growing. It was 11 o'clock.

Atop a police car outside the precinct Bob Curvin of CORE, Still, and Lofton called for a militant demonstration. Curvin declared that the police were conducting a war against the black community. Still spoke not as an official, but in his informal role of neighborhood leader, expressing anger at "sadists" in the precinct but urging the people to be peaceful. Lofton reiterated the need for an orderly demonstration, promising that all his legal resources would go to the defense of the cab-driver.

But this was one of those occasions in which people take leadership in their own hands. Although each speaker was loudly cheered, the people were in no mood to march, as certain of the organizational leaders could sense. A few marched behind Tim Still, but the line soon fell apart. A local man took the police bullhorn and simply said, "Come down the street, we got some shit." In the darkness across from the precinct young men from the neighborhood were picking up bricks and bottles, and looking for some gasoline.

13

Missiles started to fly at the precinct, where 110 windows would eventually be broken. A friend pulled Curvin away from the front of the station, and the rest of the assembled crowd moved back in anticipation of the police. The police came out with helmets and clubs but were driven back inside by a torrent of bricks and bottles. People started to move back across the street as the front of the precinct became a battle zone.

Just after midnight, two Molotov cocktails exploded high on the western wall of the precinct. A stream of fire curled fifty feet down the wall, flared for ten seconds, and died. The people, now numbering at least 500 on the street, let out a gasp of excitement. Fear, or at least caution, was apparent also as many retreated into the darkness or behind cars in the Hayes parking lot.

After three years of wondering when "the riot" would come to Newark, people knew that this could be it. While city officials pointed with pride to Newark's record of peace, most of the community knew it was only a matter of time until the explosion: "And when Newark goes," according to street wisdom, "it's going to really go."

Much of the community predicted that Newark's riot would be triggered by a police incident. While unemployment, housing and educational problems are created far from the ghetto, the police are seen as direct carriers of intimidation, harassment and violence. Dominated by the Italians who run Newark politics, tainted by alleged underworld connections, including a token of about 250 blacks among its 1400 members (all of them in subordinated positions), the police department seems to many Negroes to be an armed agency defending the privileges of the city's shrinking white community.

The police have been assertive about their rights and stature. When CORE marched against police brutality in 1965, police were heavily involved in a counterdemonstration that lasted five days and included over 5000 people. Police director Dominick Spina was outspoken against "leftist" influences in the civil rights and anti-poverty organizations. A month before the riots, he warned the Rotarians that if businessmen didn't soon become involved in the city's problems, he feared either "the fall of our civilization or a right-wing dictatorship."

The police have always been highly defensive about the brutality charge. Since 1960 they have had a complaint-taking system of their own. Of 60 complaints made in six years, the police investigators have substantiated the charge of brutality two times. In addition, although rejecting CORE's demand in 1965, for a civilian review board, the Mayor decided to refer future complaints of brutality to the FBI and county prosecutor. From September 1965 until August 1967, 7 cases were reported but no action was taken on any. The case of cab-driver Smith was the first referred to the FBI in more than a year.

15

The police were well-trained in methods of "human relations." Sophisticated crowd-control techniques were used at the hearings on the Medical School and education in May where Negroes disrupted the proceedings. The many watching police were ordered to make no arrests. In the year preceding the riot, the Justice Department funded the country's largest "police community relations" program in Newark, bringing 150 police together with 150 community residents in workshop discussions. Seven superior officers were assigned to "community relations" work before the riot, and 30 worked part-time to "avert disorder." The Police Athletic League became involved in running summer playstreet programs. Negro community leaders were invited to ride in patrol cars to observe police behavior.

Yet none of this seemed to be enough to affect the responses, real and potential, of the average officer. By early summer there were reports that many police were burning over what seemed to be a "soft line" by city officials toward militant Negro groups.

On the front lines against the police that night were the men between fifteen and twenty-five years old from the projects and the nearby avenues. They were the primary assailants and the most elusive enemy for the police. They were the force which broke open the situation in which masses of people began to participate. Few of them had ever been involved in civil-rights organizations, although some were known to

16

Student Nonviolent Coordinating Committee (SNCC) and Newark Community Union Project organizers who had worked from an office three blocks away beginning in 1965. They were friendly to the organizers, approved of the program of community organizing, but "joined" only to the extent of hanging out or playing music. They liked and understood the slogan "black power." They were "organized" on a very loose basis; Newark has no major gangs. But these youths still are capable of communicating and acting on an effective citywide basis. Phil Hutchings of SNCC described them as "young people with nothing to do and nothing to lose."

Fathers and mothers in the ghetto often complain that even they cannot understand the wildness of their kids. Knowing that America denies opportunity to black young men, black parents still share with whites the sense that youth is heading in a radically new, incomprehensible, and frightening direction. Refusal to obey authority—that of parents, teachers and other adult "supervisors"—is a common charge against youngsters. Yet when the riot broke out, the generations came together. The parents understood and approved the defiance of their sons that night.

So while the young men grouped their forces, shouted and armed themselves against the helmeted police with whatever they could find on the ground, the older generation gathered in greater and greater numbers in the rear. The Hayes projects are a useful terrain for people making war. The police station is

17

well lit, but the projects are dark, especially the rooftops a hundred yards above the street. Each room in
the projects can be darkened to allow people to observe or attack from their windows. There is little
light in the pathways, recreation areas, and parking
lots around the foot of the tall buildings. The police
thus were faced with the twin dangers of ambush and
searching through a shadow world where everybody
and everything appears to be alike. It was in this
sanctuary that parents came together. It was here also
that their sons could return to avoid the police.

Less than an hour after the bomb hit the precinct,
the looting phase began. A group of twenty-five young
people on 17th Avenue decided that the time was ripe
to break into the stores. They ran up 17th toward
Belmont as the word of their mission spread along
the way. "They're going up to Harry's," a mother
excitedly said. She and her friends looked quizzically
at each other, then started running up to the corner.
A boom and a crash signaled the opening of the new
stage. Burglar-alarm bells were ringing up and down
Belmont and 17th within fifteen minutes. People
poured out from the project areas into liquor and
furniture stores as the young people tore them open.

The police now began patrolling on foot in small
teams. It was clear that they were both outnumbered
and uncertain of themselves in the streets. Police violence began. The next day Newark Human Rights
Commission Chairman Al Black would report to the
Mayor on what the police were capable of doing when

18

"order" collapsed: a Negro policeman in civilian clothes was beaten by white policemen when he entered the Fourth Precinct to report for duty; Mrs. Vera Brinson was told to "get the hell upstairs" and hit on the neck with a club in Hayes Homes; Gregory Smith said police shouted "all you black niggers get upstairs" at project residents; two men were seized by police as they returned from work, one beaten by eight police at the precinct and the other punched and kicked by fifteen police at the entrance to his building. These people were not "criminals," Black told the Mayor, but working people.

But in the first hours the police could not control the streets in spite of nearly a hundred arrests and numerous attacks on people. After a while they developed an uneasy coexistence with the crowd, the police in twos and threes taking up positions to "protect" stores that were already looted, the people moving on to other stores. More police tried in vain to regain control of 17th Avenue and Belmont but were trapped in a pattern of frustrating advance-and-retreat.

One hope of the police may have been to keep the riot from spreading. Again, however, this was beyond their control. If they had used greater force on Belmont and 17th, the result would probably have been to spread the riot by making people move beyond the zone of fire. Furthermore, though all of Newark's 1400 police were being mobilized, it is doubtful there were enough men to cordon off a spreading mass of rioters effectively. Therefore the question of when

19

and how the riot would spread was more in the hands of the people than the police. That it did not spread may indicate the lack of real organization. All around the original riot zone people were sitting on their stoops or sleeping in their homes within earshot of the window. Yet word did not spread until the following day.

Moreover, an incident involving Smith's fellow cab-drivers Wednesday night tends to indicate that the spreading word by itself is not sufficient to spread the action. The cab-drivers were the one group equipped to let thousands of people in the city know what had happened. Within a few hours of Smith's arrest, the black cabbies were deciding by radio to meet at the precinct and form a protest caravan to City Hall. Between 1 and 2 A.M. at least twenty cars were lined up along Belmont at the corner of 17th, creating new noise, excitement, and fury. After nearly an hour of waiting and planning, the cabs roared down to police headquarters, located behind City Hall, to demand release of Smith. They carried close to a hundred passengers from the riot area with them. At head-quarters they were able to secure a promise that Smith would be adequately treated and released after arraignment in the morning. At the same time the police closed off traffic on Broad Street in front of City Hall, thus helping further to alert citizens who had not been affected by the rioting or the cab-drivers' caravan. Police by this time were swinging their clubs freely, even at confused motorists, perhaps out of fear

20

that bombs would be thrown against the City Hall building itself.

Yet the riot did not spread. At 4 A.M. most of the participants had gone home. About fifty people, mostly young, stood on the corner of 17th and Fairview watching and occasionally taunting police who had "secured" 17th Avenue. Police cars and wagons patrolled up and down 17th; now and then, policemen would leap out of their cars to charge at the people on the corner, only to watch them vanish up alleys and between houses. By 5 A.M. everyone had vanished from the streets, except the police.

Newark's officials must have viewed the riot as a plague for which there were no doctors, no medicine. In this sense they were right: there was no one with whom they could deal or bargain. A week after the riot a Newark official told the New York *Daily News* (July 21):

> After the first night of rioting, the Mayor spent all day trying to get through to the kids. He was making contact with the adults and adult leaders, but who was speaking for the kids? We couldn't even understand what demand they had.

Exactly.

II

▼

Thursday:
The Community Takes Over

THURSDAY morning's paper denied what everyone knew was true. Mayor Addonizio called the events of the previous evening an "isolated incident," not of genuine riot proportions. In their behavior, however, city officials gave plenty of indication that they were worried.

The Mayor called in civil rights leaders, including both moderate ministers and some of his more militant opponents. Concessions were made. Addonizio decided to ask for City Council funds to allow additional police captaincies so that a qualified Negro officer, Eddie Williams, could become the first Negro captain. He requested that Human Rights Director James Threatt and Police Director Dominick Spina separately investigate Wednesday's conflict. He re-

23

assigned the two patrolmen who beat Smith to "administrative positions." He referred the Smith case to the county prosecutor and FBI. He announced formation of a Blue Ribbon Commission, like the McCone Commission that investigated Watts, to examine this "isolated incident." The Mayor was doing what militant politicians were demanding. But when someone told him point blank that the people had lost confidence in his administration, Addonizio replied: "That's politics. Sit down. You've said enough."

There was no civil rights leader, no organization, capable of determining what was to come. Sensing this, some community activists refused to engage in what they felt were fruitless meetings downtown. Others tried to warn the Mayor of what might happen in full knowledge that the Mayor was now powerless. Others worked desperately for a proposal that could be brought to the community in an effort to bargain for peace. Many jockeyed for position, worrying about who had the Mayor's ear, who might be blamed, who would be the channel for resources from the establishment to the community.

Some community activists settled on the idea of a demonstration in the evening at the precinct. At a neighborhood anti-poverty center near the precinct, they ran off a leaflet that said simply: "Stop! Police Brutality!" It would be given out to motorists, calling a 7:30 demonstration at the precinct. Some organizers of this demonstration probably thought it might

24

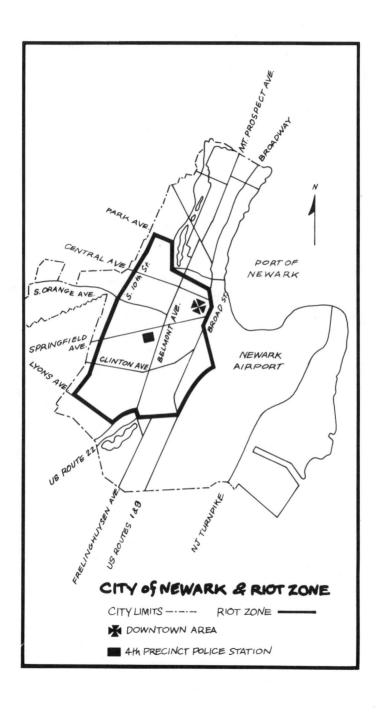

MT. PROSPECT AVE.

BROADWAY

PARK AVE.

CENTRAL AVE.

PORT OF
NEWARK

S. 10th St.

S. ORANGE AVE.

BELMONT AVE.

BROAD ST.

SPRINGFIELD
AVE.

CLINTON AVE.

NEWARK
AIRPORT

LYONS AVE.

US ROUTE 22

FRELINGHUYSEN AVE.

US ROUTES 1&9

NJ TURNPIKE

CITY OF NEWARK & RIOT ZONE

CITY LIMITS —·—·—   RIOT ZONE ————

✠ DOWNTOWN AREA

■ 4th PRECINCT POLICE STATION

channel energy away from violence. Others knew the violence was there, not to be channeled into symbolic protest, yet conventional protest was the only avenue of expression familiar to them. So they proceeded. Police Director Spina would later claim this activity helped "fuel" the explosion later that night.

Regardless of what the Mayor did, regardless of what civil rights leaders did, regardless of what planners of the demonstration did, the riot was going to happen. The authorities had been indifferent to the community's demand for justice; now the community was going to be indifferent to the authorities' demand for order. This was apparent to community organizers who walked around the projects Thursday afternoon talking to young people. All the organizers urged was that burning of buildings be minimized so as to spare lives.

Meanwhile the leaflets were going out as planned. By late afternoon about twenty-five people were picketing the precinct, mostly young kids. By 6 P.M. a somewhat larger number were picketing in the street where traffic had been blocked off. More than a hundred people gathered in the parking lot of the projects. An equal number lined 17th Avenue on both sides. These were people of the community. Almost no one from the poverty program or existing organizations was involved in leading the pickets. An Afro drum group arrived and started playing.

Word spread. At a bar five blocks away, for example, people heard the news and started for 17th Avenue. Only one out of the twenty-five or so remained behind; he didn't want a riot to break out because in his view, one inevitable result of a riot would be that Negro prisoners in the jail he had just left would be beaten.

Back at the precinct where the tempo was increasing by the minute, Human Rights Commission Director James Threatt arrived with a message to the crowd from the Mayor. Threatt said Addonizio promised a Negro police captain by July 17 if the demonstration would stop. People told Threatt to get off the precinct steps where he was standing. A Negro detective possibly FBI agent John Randall who was identified in the *New York Times,* July 14, started moving back the crowd now surrounding Threatt. When he failed, several community activists cleared the stairs. Another Negro detective then stood on the steps to ask "Why don't you people just go home?" Someone threw an object at him, but the man did not move. Rocks and bottles started flying. The detective was pulled out of the way, then rocks and bottles were thrown at the precinct. A lady in white started punching out precinct windows with a stick.

David Crooms, a black free-lance photographer, was on the scene. "The rioting would have broken out anyway," he believes, but it began at the precinct when the demonstration was disrupted by Threatt's appearance with the empty offer. With other press

27

members, Crooms moved across the street to the gas station. There he heard one officer inside the station yelling "When the hell are we going out there?" Then the side door opened. Crooms tells this story:

> Big white cops came out yelling "Let's go get these mother-fuckers." Myself and the other newsmen, four of them, ran along behind the charging police. We followed them out to the court in the middle of Hayes Homes. On the way, they caught one black newsman off to the side and beat him. They chased this colored fellow who was running in the court. Twelve or fourteen cops got on him, dropped him, and beat him. We were still behind the cops. Next thing I knew, one yelled, "get that black mother-fucker." The rest of the newsmen stood and wondered what was going on. There were no questions asked. They hit me on top of the head, and I went out for maybe five seconds. When I came to, one of them hit me just below the eye. They ran off. I went back to the precinct. The captain said he was sorry and told me to file a complaint.

Al Black, the chairman of the Newark Human Rights Commission, was around the Fourth Precinct from 7 that evening to 3:30 the next morning. He heard the police "using vicious racial slurs on Negroes, including calling them black S.O.B.'s." He saw police beating young Negroes under arrest as they were being taken to the precinct. Police dragged in Negroes with their hands handcuffed behind their backs while other officers were striking them with night-

28

sticks on the head and on the body. "I tried to prevent the police from beating Negroes they arrested. I demanded that the police take jailed persons who were bleeding profusely to the hospital and they complied." Director Spina was inside the station.

Heavy looting soon began on Springfield Avenue, three blocks from the precinct, the largest commercial street in the ghetto. By midnight there was action everywhere in the ghetto although the Mayor announced that the disturbance was being brought to an end. Partly the expansion was caused by people moving in new directions outward from the looted areas where police were concentrated. Partly it was people in new neighborhoods following the example of people in the original area. A human network of communication was forming, with people in the streets its main conductors.

The youth were again in the lead, breaking windows where the chance appeared, chanting "Black Power," moving in groups through dark streets to new commercial areas. This was more than a case of youth stepping in where parents feared to tread. This was the largest demonstration of black people ever held in Newark. At any major intersection, and there are at least ten such points in the ghetto, there were more than a thousand people on the streets at the same time. A small number entered stores and moved out with what they could carry; they would be replaced by others from the large mass of people walking, running, or standing in the streets. Further

29

back were more thousands who watched from windows and stoops and periodically participated. Those with mixed feelings were not about to intervene against their neighbors. A small number, largely the older people, shook their heads.

People voted with their feet to expropriate property to which they felt entitled. They were tearing up the stores with the trick contracts and installment plans, the second-hand television sets going for top-quality prices, the phony scales, the inferior meat and vegetables. A common claim was: this is owed me. But few needed to argue. People who under ordinary conditions respected law because they were forced to do so now felt free to act upon the law as they thought it should be. When an unpopular store was opened up, with that mighty crash of glass or ripping sound of metal, great shouts of joy would sound. "Hey, they got Alice's!" "They gave that place what he deserved." "They did? G-o-o-d!"

The riot was more effective against gouging merchants than organized protest had ever been. The year before a survey was started to check on merchants who weighted their scales. The survey collapsed because of disinterest: people needed power, not proof. This spring the welfare mothers spent a month planning and carrying out a protest against a single widely hated store. The owner finally was forced to close his business, but only after nineteen people were arrested in a demonstration. There was no effective follow-up against the other stores, though frightened merchants cleaned up their stores, offered bribes to organizers, and chipped in money to outfit a kid's baseball team. But it was too late for concessions.

The Negro middle class and "respectable" working people participated heavily on Thursday night. Well-dressed couples with kids in their car were a common sight. One woman who said she already could afford the "junk" sold in the ghetto decided to wait until the rioting spread to fancier sections where she could get expensive furs. Doubtless the Mayor's failure to act on issues such as education caused disaffection among the black middle class. Doubtless, too, the middle class willingness to consider rioting legitimate made it more likely that a riot would happen.

But it is doubtful that any tactics by the Mayor could have divided the black middle class from the ghetto in such a way as to prevent a riot. The poor were going to riot. The middle class could join. Many did, because their racial consciousness cut through middle-class values to make property destruction seem reasonable, especially when the white authorities cannot see who is looting. During the Watts riot the story was told of a black executive who regularly stopped to throw bricks before attending suburban cocktail parties and barbeques; the same attitude was present in Newark. When police systematically attacked Negro-owned stores later in the week, they were only confirming what the black middle class, reluctantly, was starting to understand: that racism ultimately makes no distinction between "proper" and "lowly" colored people.

Black unity, solidarity, spirit, the feeling of being home: by whatever name the fact was plain. There is no question whether the majority of Negroes gave support. People on the street felt free to take shelter from the police in homes of people they did not know. What concerned Governor Hughes greatly the next morning was the "carnival atmosphere" of people looting even in daylight. What for Hughes seemed like "laughing at a funeral" was to many in the community more like the celebration of a new beginning. People felt as though for a moment they were creating a community of their own.

Economic gain was the basis of mass involvement. The stores presented the most immediate way for people to take what they felt was theirs. Liquor was the most convenient item to steal. The Governor's announcement on Friday morning that he would "dry the town out" came a little late. But liquor was hardly the sole object of the looters. Boys who had few clothes took home more than they had ever owned before. Mattresses were carried into apartments to replace the second-hand or over-used ones purchased on installment. New television sets, irons, tables and chairs, baseball bats, dishware and other household goods were carried out in armloads. People walked, ran, or drove off with their possessions. There were Negro gangsters and hi-jackers, with connections in the white mob network, on the scene too, but most of the people were taking only for themselves. One reason there was so little quarrelling over "who gets what" was that there was, for a change, enough for all.

For the most part the rioting was controlled and focussed. The "rampaging" was aimed almost exclusively at white-owned stores, and not at such buildings as schools, churches, or banks. The latter institutions are oppressive but their buildings contain little that can be carried off. To this extent the riot was concrete rather than symbolic. There were no attacks by Negroes on "soul brother" stores. There were people injured by glass on the streets where they fell, but they typically fell because police chased them, not because of stampeding into each other in the rush for goods.

Basic feelings of racial hate were released at white people far less often than was suggested by the media. Many missiles were thrown at cars driven by whites but not often with murderous intent. Several times such cars were stopped, the occupants jeered at and terrified, and a few actual beatings occurred. However, no white passers-by or store owners were killed and very few, if any, were shot at. No white neighborhoods were attacked, though rioting reached the borders of at least four separate white areas. Several white community workers felt able to move around on foot freely by day and even at night, especially in the company of Negroes. Driving was

33

more difficult because all white people appeared to be outsiders. These conditions remained the same throughout the week, though the tensions between whites and blacks intensified as the stage of spirited looting was replaced by that of bitter confrontation with the troops.

Police behavior became more and more violent as the looting expanded. The size of the rebellion was far too large for 1400 patrolmen. Their tactic seemed to be to drive at high speeds, with sirens whining, down major streets in the ghetto. Thus they were driving too fast for rock-throwers while still attempting a show of force. As a result of this maneuver a woman was run down and apparently killed on 17th Avenue. The sight and sound of the police also stirred the community into greater excitement.

As darkness fell, the number of arrests increased sharply. Police started firing blanks. According to the *New York Times* of July 14, police were asking by radio for "the word" to shoot, and when news came in that policemen in one car were shooting real bullets, another voice shouted over the radio: "It's about time; give them hell." At midnight orders were given for police to use "all necessary means—including firearms—to defend themselves."

Murdering looters now was possible. A short time afterwards, twenty-eight-year-old Tedock Bell walked out of his Bergen Street home to see what had happened to the nearby bar where he was employed.

34

When the police came, his wife left in fright. But Tedock told his sister-in-law and her boyfriend not to run because they weren't doing anything. They did run, however, while he walked. He became the first victim a minute later.

About 4 A.M. two patrolmen reported they saw four men emerge with bottles from a liquor store on Jones Street. They called halt, the officers told the Newark *News*—calling halt is a prerequisite to shooting someone—but the looters ran. One was shot and killed going through a fence.

More than 250 people were treated at City Hospital that night, at least fifteen reportedly for gunshot wounds. Less than one-quarter of them were held for further diagnosis and treatment. The police took over the ambulances from the Negro drivers and rescue workers. Snipers were shooting at the ambulances, police said. By 2:20 A.M. Mayor Addonizio was revising his midnight estimate that the situation was under control. Announcing that things had deteriorated, he asked Governor Hughes for aid in restoring order.

By early morning Friday 425 people were in jail. In addition to five dead, hundreds were wounded or injured. The Newark *News* that morning expressed hope that Newark might again become a city "in which people can live and work harmoniously in a climate that will encourage, not repel, the expansion of the business industry that provide jobs for all." In the *Star-Ledger's* opinion, there was a need for community leaders "to act with dispatch to putting to rest false reports that sometimes touch off violent transgressions."

III

↓

The Occupation

"An obvious open rebellion," asserted Governor Hughes after his tour of Newark at 5 A.M. Friday. From that announcement until Monday afternoon, the black community was under military occupation. More than 3000 National Guardsmen were called up Friday morning from the surrounding white suburbs and southern Jersey towns. Five hundred white state troopers arrived at the same time. By mid-afternoon Friday they were moving in small convoys throughout the city, both clockwise and counter-clockwise, circling around seven parts of the ghetto. Guardsmen were moving in jeeps or small open trucks, usually led or followed by carloads of troopers or Newark police. Bayonets were attached to the Guards' .30-caliber M-1 rifles or .30-caliber carbines, which they carried in addition to .45-caliber pistols. Personnel carriers weighing as much as eleven tons, and trucks mounted with machine guns, appeared here and there among the jeeps and police cars. The presence of these vehicles was designed, according to Governor Hughes, to build the confidence of the Negro community.

Confidence in what? Hughes defined the issues over and over in television, radio, and press interviews, as well as in meetings with community leaders. "The line between the jungle and the law might as well be drawn here as any place in America," he announced shortly after arriving. On Saturday he talked again of the line between society and the jungle, adding that the Negroes "had better choose sides" because the "side of law and order has joined this to the finish."

Certainly the police and much of white America agreed. In the carrying out of the Governor's weekend definitions and policies at least 20 Negroes died, nearly all from police shooting, another 1000 were injured and 1000 jailed; as many as 100 Negro-owned businesses were attacked by police and troopers; and hundreds of apartments were fired into along the ghetto's streets. The average white citizen was convinced that these things had to be done in order to halt what Governor Hughes called a "criminal insurrection." The troops, the public was told, had to be brought in to put an end to the looting, burning, and sniping. *But did the troops really carry out these purposes?*

The police themselves reported that looting was on the decline when the troops arrived: "the police radio which put out alarms at a frantic pace Thursday night," said Saturday's Newark *News,* "was less hectic last night, but a majority of calls were for sniping." Most of the looting was at an end. When Hughes spoke of the "funeral of the city" Friday morning, he referred to the visible fact that most of the ghetto's stores were destroyed by that time. Certainly, this was true of those stores that contained merchandise that could be carried away. Nearly all the damage had been done in twelve hours Thursday night. If the troops had been concerned to prevent looting, they could have grouped themselves so as to protect the business districts downtown and in white neighborhoods. If they had wanted to protect the remaining ghetto stores, they could have stood in small teams with machine guns in front of these stores, but the fact is that they were patrolling aggressively against *people* inside the ghetto.

If the troops were supposed to prevent stores from burning, they were not needed. A motoring caravan of troops cannot prevent people from setting a building on fire, nor are troops equipped to fight blazes already set. Nor could they do much to shield firemen from missiles that are thrown, dropped, or fired. Moreover, the facts show that arson was insignificant in the Newark riot. Although the fire department reported 110 alarms from Thursday afternoon to Friday morning, it later admitted that most of the alarms were false; and a drive through the city on Friday morning showed evidence of no more than twenty-five fires throughout the ghetto. There was a clear reason for this: most of the houses are wood-frame firetraps, and Negroes live above most of the stores that were looted. Burning would have risked the lives and property of black people. At the end of the riot, the fire department figures showed only ten "major" fires.

But the major justification for the use of troops, especially as looting and burning diminished, was the need to counter the attacks of snipers. There were 3000 National Guardsmen, 1400 Newark police, 500 state troopers, and several hundred firemen who were standing and riding in the open during the riot. They were exposed, it was claimed, to a "withering sniper fire." With a pistol, or certainly with a rifle, a single amateur sniper could have killed several policemen. But only one policeman and one fireman were killed, both *after* the troops were brought in. The circumstances of their deaths are unclear. Both were described as sniper victims, although they were caught in the middle of police fire, and no one knew even the direction from which the snipers were shooting. But even if we assume they were sniper victims, two killings from Wednesday to Monday, in an area swarming with troops, suggest that the sniper fire from Negroes was far more limited than was claimed.

Life published an interview with a sniper who said that few whites were killed because the snipers were shooting in the air in order to distract the police from looters. If this was so, the officials who reported direct and heavy fire on police cars, ambulances, fire trucks, jeeps, and armored cars were being less than accurate about a very important issue. A shot in the air can be distinguished from withering fire aimed at human targets or vehicles.

No snipers were killed. No one was arrested in the act of sniping. Many people in the community knew that guns and ammunition were around, but only a tiny handful of people did any shooting. Some of these were isolated individuals, some operated in small groups. However, it must be emphasized that it was impossible for the snipers to initiate the riot. In the judgment of those who were present at the crucial incident on Wednesday, July 12, none of the people who could be considered "organized snipers" were even on the scene. They only began to emerge on Thursday after large numbers of young people had made their decision to riot. It is entirely possible that the riot would have been over if the troops had not entered the community on Friday afternoon. The snipers were the pretext used by officials to commit thousands of violent acts against the whole Negro community. If the Governor was concerned about snipers, people in the ghetto said, then he should not have sent in the troops who served as targets.

But the troops came flooding in. John V. Spinale, an assistant to the Governor, stated that they had been instructed to act with the "utmost restraint" and to "shoot only when necessary, primarily in self-defense." The reality was very different.

In the heavily looted Clinton Hill area (to take one example), the troops arrived early Friday afternoon. Parking their tank, armored cars, and jeeps in a lot ordinarily used by shoppers, the troops made their way up and down the avenue brandishing rifles and bayonets. Hundreds of people were on the street before they came, mostly people looking in wonder at the shattered remains of stores. When the troops arrived, however, young people and men came to the avenue in larger numbers than before. To show the troops that securing the area was impossible by military means, several youths set fire to a store the soldiers were "guarding." Several fire engines and troop reinforcements rushed to the scene, drawing thousands of people onto the street. Periodically squads of soldiers would march down the street driving people away with outstretched bayonets. But when the clearance was over, the people returned.

As dusk came, about fifty Guardsmen and troopers took up positions on the four corners of Clinton and Hunterdon. Several of them stood in the center of the street directing pedestrian and automobile traffic. Along Hunterdon Street people lined the stoops and stood in front of their homes. About thirty men, mostly young, stayed around the corner, alternately talking and arguing with the troops. The troops were all white, a fact that was not lost on one person who shouted that her son was in Vietnam.

At one point a car bearing Newark police drove down Hunterdon. A curse was uttered at the car by a man on the stoops, and the policeman slammed to a halt. The driver backed the car up to where the man was standing, stopped, got out, and approached the man wrapping the leather cord of the nightstick around his wrist. "What did you say? What did you say, Mister?" the club grazing back and forth over the motionless black face. "Do you want this over your head? Well, get back inside. Do you hear me, get back inside. Get inside your house!" The policeman's eyes were bulging and his voice was trembling. The man backed up to his porch, the policeman backed up to his car. Two hundred people had formed into a quiet audience.

When the police drove away, the young men went back up Hunterdon to taunt the Guardsmen. The soldiers marched toward them, bayonets pointing. The kids kept coming, a few spreading out into the street or behind the cars. Face to face, ten soldiers with guns against twenty-five kids with two bottles. The Guardsmen pushed the kids back with their bayonets. One bayonet went too far through the shirt and the victim turned around screaming into the soldier's face. Quickly the troops circled around him, and the rest of the kids moved into a wider circle. With the bayonet jabbing his skin, the young man continued yelling. Down the street troopers rushed with pistols and clubs swinging. The soldiers opened their circle to allow the trooper to crack the captured one across the back. Two blows and he fell to the street, and twisted in a convulsion. Rocks and bottles flew at the troops and four black men ran up to the writhing body. They sat on the victim to prevent his body from snapping. At the corner all the Guardsmen were in a square formation pointing their rifles at people along the street and in their houses. They marched around in a tight step. The people retreated into homes and alleys. The street fell silent except for the soldiers' footfalls. A neighborhood worker, encouraged by the police to cool people off, put down his bullhorn and swore. "If they're going to do this, fuck it. I can't do anything." After a moment he picked up the bullhorn and started speaking: "Please, people, take your little children inside, take your children inside. Someone is going to get hurt out here."

IV

▼

The Terror

WE WILL NEVER know the full story of how these troops and the police hurt the black people of Newark. But there is now sufficient evidence to establish the main features of their behavior.

The military forces called in to put down the black rebellion were nearly all white. Virtually none of the 250 Negro Newark policemen took part directly in the violent suppression. Only 1.2 per cent of the New Jersey National Guard is black and, according to columnists Evans and Novak on July 22, the organization is "highly social in nature—much like the local chapter of the Moose or Elks. Few Negroes ever try to join." There are five Negroes among 1200 New Jersey state troopers, and many of the white majority are from conservative South Jersey towns where the troopers act as local police. It was understandable that these men would bring into the ghetto racist attitudes that would soon support outright sadism. A captain who commanded helicopter-borne infantry told a *New York Times* reporter on July 14:

> They put us here because we're the toughest and the best . . . If anybody throws things down our necks, then it's shoot to kill, it's either them or us, and it ain't going to be us.

On Saturday the 15th, troopers charged up the stairs of the Hayes Homes, shouting, "Get back, you black niggers!" There was shooting up each flight of stairs as they charged. Later, an officer pumped more than thirty bullets into the body of a fallen teen-ager while shouting, "Die, bastard, die!" A Guardsman asked a witness, "What do you want us to do, kill all you Negroes?" A Newark policeman chipped in, "We are going to do it anyway, so we might as well take care of these three now."

These are not isolated examples, but a selection from innumerable incidents of the kind that were reported throughout the riots. From them, we can draw three conclusions about the soldiers and the police.

Trigger-Happiness Because of Fear, Confusion and Exhaustion: Many of the troops were assigned to round-the-clock duty. During that duty they were under conditions of extreme tension. They were kept moving about by incidents or reports of looting, burning and shooting. They drove at speeds of more

46

than 50 miles per hour; they ran continually along the streets after people. They were surrounded by unfamiliar and hostile faces. There were no foxholes or other shelters from attack. The troopers and Guardsmen knew little or nothing about the terrain. They often were unable to tell the direction of shooting. The New York *Daily News* of July 20 summarized:

> Reporters in the riot area feared the random shots of the guardsmen far more than the shots from snipers . . . Once a frantic voice shouted [over the radio], "Tell those Guardsmen to stop shooting at the roof. Those men they're firing at are policemen." . . . "They were completely out of their depth," said one reporter. "It was like giving your kid brother a new toy. They were firing at anything and everything."

In a report on police behavior for the *New York Times* July 20, Peter Khiss quoted the police radio on Sunday night to this effect:

> Newark police, hold your fire! State police, hold your fire! . . . You're shooting at each other! National Guardsmen, you're shooting at buildings and sparks fly so we think there are snipers! Be sure of your targets!

Khiss adds: "After these appeals, there seemed to be a decrease in sniper alarms."

General and Deliberate Violence Employed Against

the Whole Community: On Friday night 10 Negroes were killed, 100 suffered gunshot wounds, 500 were "treated" at City Hospital, and at least as many were arrested or held. By Sunday night another 10 were dead, at least 50 more had gunshot wounds, and another 500 were in jail. People were stopped indiscriminately in the streets, shoved, cursed, and beaten and shot. On Thursday, Joe Price, a veteran of the Korean war and an employee of ITT for fifteen years, was beaten on the head, arms, stomach and legs by five Newark policemen inside the Fourth Precinct. He had protested police harassment of neighborhood teen-agers earlier in the day. Later, Jerry Berfet, walking peacefully on a sidewalk with two women, was stopped by the police who told him to strip, ripped off his clothes, and forced him to run naked down the street. No charges were entered against either man. A Negro professional worker was arrested while driving on a quiet street after the 10 P.M. curfew, beaten unconscious, and then forced to perform what his lawyer describes as "degrading acts" when he revived in the police station.

Troops fired freely and wildly up streets and into buildings at real or imagined enemies.

On Saturday before darkness fell, three women were killed in their homes by police fire. Rebecca Brown, a twenty-nine-year-old nurse's aide, was cut nearly in half as she tried to rescue her two-year-old child by the window. Hattie Gainer, an elderly twenty-year resident of her neighborhood, was shot at her window in view of her three grandchildren. Eloise Spellman was shot through the neck in her Hayes apartment with three of her eleven children present.

A child in Scudder Homes lost his ear and eye to a bullet. A man was shot while fixing his car as police charged after a crowd. When another man told police he was shot in the side, the officer knocked him down and kicked him in the ribs.

The most obvious act of deliberate aggression was the police destruction of perhaps a hundred Negro-owned stores Saturday and Sunday. One witness followed police down Bergen Street for fifteen blocks watching them shoot into windows marked "soul brother." Another store owner observed a systematic pattern. On his block three white-owned stores were looted Thursday night; no Negro stores were damaged. There were no other disturbances on his block until well after midnight Saturday when he received calls that troopers were shooting into the Negro-owned stores or were breaking windows with the butts of their guns.

Was it because the police hated black people indiscriminately? Was it because the police wanted to teach middle-class Negroes that they must take responsibility for what "criminal" Negroes do? Or because the police wanted to prevent Negro-operated stores from gaining an advantage over the looted white merchants? Whatever the reason, the result was summed up clearly by Gustav Heningburg, a Negro who is a lay official of the Episcopal Church. He told the Newark *News* of July 17 that "the non-rioting Negroes are more afraid of the police than the rioters" because the police were retaliating instead of protecting.

Governor Hughes said on Sunday that all reports of excessive behavior would be handled by the troopers' own investigative unit. If charges were proved true, "and after all the police are only human," the Governor was sure that "justice will be done." As for himself, "I felt a thrill of pride in the way our state police and National Guardsmen have conducted themselves."

Cold-Blooded Murder: An evaluation of the deaths so far reported suggests that the military forces killed people for the purposes of terror and intimidation. Nearly all the dead were killed by police, troopers, and Guardsmen. The "crimes" of the victims were petty, vague, or unproven. None were accused by police of being snipers; only one so far is alleged to have been carrying a gun. Several of the dead were engaged in small-scale looting at most. The majority were observers; ten, in fact, were killed inside or just outside their homes. Many were killed in daylight. Nearly all the dead had families and jobs; only a few had previous criminal records. Seven of the dead were women, two were young boys. Of those known to be dead, 5 were killed between Thursday night and dawn Friday: 1 in a hit-and-run car, 1 allegedly shot by mistake by a sniper, 3 others

50

by Newark police. On Friday and Friday night 9 were slain; 9 between Saturday afternoon and late Sunday; 1 on Monday night. All but one or two of these seemed to be police victims.

The July 28th issue of *Life* magazine carried a photo-essay on the death of William Furr. On Saturday afternoon Furr and a few others were carrying cases of beer out of a store that had been looted the previous night. Furr appears in the *Life* photos in the act of looting. The *Life* reporter even shared a can of stolen beer, and was warned by Furr to "get rid of it and run like hell" if the police appeared. Suddenly the police raced up with their sirens off, jumped out of the car with shotguns. Furr, according to the *Life* article, had "part of a six-pack in his left hand." With the *Life* photographer's camera shutter snapping, William Furr ran halfway down the block before two shots from behind dropped him. He died almost immediately, and a twelve-year-old boy, Joe Bass, was severely wounded while standing at the end of the block. A few minutes before Furr had told the *Life* reporter, "When the police treat us like people instead of treating us like animals, then the riots will stop."

The killing of nineteen-year-old James Rutledge will not soon be forgotten in Newark. On Sunday afternoon, he was inside a looted tavern with several other teen-agers hiding from the fire of troopers and police. According to a witness, the troopers burst into the tavern shooting and yelling, "Come out you dirty fucks." James Rutledge agreed to come out from behind a cigarette machine. He was frisked against the wall. Then:

> The two troopers . . . looked at each other. Then one trooper who had a rifle shot Jimmy from about three feet away . . . While Jimmy lay on the floor, the same trooper started to shoot Jimmy some more with the rifle. As he fired . . . he yelled "Die, you dirty bastard, die you dirty nigger, die, die . . ." At this point a Newark policeman walked in and asked what happened. I saw the troopers look at each other and smile . . .
>
> The trooper who shot Jimmy remained . . . took a knife out of his own pocket and put it in Jimmy's hand.
>
> Shortly after three men came in with a stretcher. One said, "they really laid some lead on his ass" . . . He asked the state trooper what happened. The trooper said, "He came at me with a knife" . . .
>
> [We remained where we were] for about fifteen minutes, then I got up and walked to the window and knocked a board down. —— and —— came over to the window. One state trooper and two National Guardsmen came to the window and said, "Come out or we are going to start shooting" . . .
>
> A National Guardsman said, "What do you want us to do, kill all you Negroes?" I saw a Newark policeman say: "We are going to do it anyway, we might as well take care of these three now." I saw the Newark policeman go over to——, point a pistol at his head and say: "How do you feel?" Then he started laughing . . .

For anyone who wonders whether this is an exaggerated youthful horror story, the photographs of James Rutledge's chest and head are available from his mother. There were forty-five bulletholes in his head and body.

Clearly the evidence points to a military massacre and suppression in Newark rather than to a two-sided war. This was not only the conclusion of the Negroes in the ghetto but of private Newark lawyers, professors of constitutional law and representatives of the state American Civil Liberties Union. They have charged that the police were the instrument of a conspiracy "to engage in a pattern of systematic violence, terror, abuse, intimidation, and humiliation" to keep Negroes second-class citizens. The police, according to the lawyers' statement, "seized on the initial disorders as an opportunity and pretext to perpetrate the most horrendous and widespread killing, violence, torture, and intimidation, not in response to any crime or civilian disorder, but as a violent demonstration of the powerlessness of the plaintiffs and their class . . ."

Thus it seems to many that the military, especially the Newark police, not only triggered the riot by beating a cab-driver but then created a climate of opinion that supported the use of all necessary force to suppress the riot. The force used by police was not in response to snipers, looting, and burning, but in retaliation against the successful uprising of Wednesday and Thursday nights.

The action of the troops was supported by civilian

authority, which turned the legal and judicial process into an anti-riot weapon. "New Jersey will show its abhorrence of these criminal activities and society will protect itself by fair, speedy and retributive justice," the Governor declared. Not counting hundreds of Negroes swept up by police, held for hours, and released without being charged, 1400 altogether were arrested and detained in jail. Of 829 adults and 144 juveniles interviewed in jail by lawyers during the riot period, more than 80 per cent were charged with looting. Nearly all the other arrests were for minor offenses such as curfew violation. Almost none were for shooting, bombing or arson.* Only 85 "dangerous weapons" were confiscated, according to final police reports, and of these only 51 were guns. About 675 of the arrested people—not quite half of them—were reported to have criminal records. But *Life* magazine

---

* An earlier, preliminary, breakdown of arrests revealed the following: 473 arrested for breaking and entering (looting, larceny); 50 for curfew violation; 47 for possession or receiving stolen goods; 40 for concealed weapons or possession of weapons; 12 for assault and battery on police, troopers, or guards; 14 for assault and battery (presumably against civilians); 9 for disorderly conduct; 14 for loitering; 3 for failure to give good account of self; 3 for resisting arrest; 3 for resisting arrest after curfew; 1 for unlawfully eluding police; 3 for auto theft; 3 for malicious damage; 3 for possession of marijuana; 2 for failure to obey a policeman; 1 for shooting wife; 1 for impersonating a member of the armed forces; 1 as a material witness; 1 for possession of a gas bomb; 1 for attempted armed robbery; 1 for discharging weapon; 3 for attempted arson; 1 for arson.

54

called this figure "somewhat loaded" since city officials admitted that in half the 675 cases the "criminal records" consisted of arrests but not convictions. The evidence is that most of the prisoners were adults with jobs and families; holding them for several days created serious problems for each.

High bail prevented prisoners from being able to get out of jail. Minimum bond was set at $1,000 for curfew and loitering charges, $2,500 for looting, $5,000 for possession of a gun, $10,000 to $25,000 for other weapons charges. Chief Magistrate James Del Mauro, replying to criticism of the high bail cost, declared in the July 14 Newark *News*: "If they can't afford it, let them stay in jail." As Henry diSuvero of the state American Civil Liberties Union pointed out, this meant that the concept of "innocent until proven guilty" and the constitutional provision against "excessive bail" was discarded. Thus people were kept off the streets and, in diSuvero's view, held as "hostages" in the conflict.

During this mass detention no one with the exception of about 150 juveniles, was fed until Saturday and many not until Sunday, even when food was brought to the jails by friends and relatives of the prisoners. As the court pens filled up, prisoners were sent to the Newark Street Jail (condemned as uninhabitable in the 1930s), federal detention facilities, a state prison, and the armory where Hughes and the troops were headquartered. Some of the prisoners were beaten in their cells.

Prisoners were not permitted to receive visitors or make telephone calls for legal assistance, nor were they allowed to notify friends and relatives. The right to preliminary hearings was denied. This right, provided for in New Jersey law, compels the prosecutor to demonstrate to the judge there is "probable cause" to hold the accused; it permits the defendant to discover the state's case against himself as well. Thus, merely the word of the arresting officer became sufficient to hold people without determination of probable cause.

Municipal Court judges started arraigning prisoners at round-the-clock sessions. One prisoner passed through court every three minutes, according to the *Star-Ledger* of July 16. Pleas by attorneys for the reduction of bail were ignored except in rare instances.

Starting Monday two Grand Juries heard felony charges and returned, by week's end, some 500 indictments. With the handing down of an indictment, which itself is a finding of probable cause, the prisoners lost forever their right to preliminary hearing. Thus, by agreeing to rush presentations, the Grand Jury acted more as a rubber stamp for the prosecutors' requests than a body to ensure an objective check on evidence. The ACLU charge that Hughes was using the judiciary as a weapon to restore order is supported by this post-riot statement the Governor gave to *US News & World Report:*

The full measure of the criminal law should be exacted in these cases. I have insisted on that from the beginning. I went to the extent of arranging with the appropriate courts for the immediate impaneling of grand juries and presentation of cases to them.

But the attitude of the courts was perhaps better indicated on July 21 when Newark's Chief Magistrate Del Mauro rejected the attempt by cab-driver Smith's attorney, Harris David, to file criminal complaints against the two police who arrested Smith. According to the *Times,* Del Mauro's words were:

> In these times of stress, with all the havoc and destruction, a policeman killed, a fireman killed, more than twenty people killed and $15 million of damage, *I am not accepting a complaint against the police.*
>
> It was this particular man, if I recall from reading the papers, that originally caused the rioting, when he was arrested and rumors swept through the colored community that he had been killed. He has been paroled . . . he is alive and there is nothing wrong with him.

"Mr. Smith," the *Times* reported the next day, "wore a six-inch-wide bandage wrapped tightly around his rib cage" and declined any comment on the advice of his lawyer.

One of the riot's lessons was that the white community, at the highest official levels, gave support to this entire military operation. The Governor stated the necessity of "drawing the line" for all America in Newark; the Governor commented he was "thrilled" by the performance of the troops; the Governor dismissed police brutality charges as "standard operating procedure." City officials were just as implicated. The *Washington Post* of July 24 reported: "There was massive destruction of property —but no deaths—until Newark Mayor Hugh J. Addonizio instructed the city police to use any means necessary to put down the riot . . ." During the height of bloodshed, when Richard Taliaferro was shot in the back on South 8th Street Friday night (the police claimed Taliaferro exchanged shots with them), the Mayor told a Newark *News* reporter: "That's a good show of force in quick time." From the streets to the court room, Negroes' rights were secondary.

In the aftermath of the riot it became clear that substantial citizens of Newark were aware of the magnitude of the police brutality issue. A Committee of Concern, including the Episcopal Bishop, the dean of Rutgers' Newark branch and the dean of Rutgers' Law School, the vice-presidents of the Prudential Insurance Company and of Newark's largest department store, declared that one of the major causes of the riot was the feeling among Negroes that the police are the "single continuously lawless element operating in the community." The solid citizens agreed that this Negro view had merit; indeed, they said "independent observers" agreed with it. Since their statement implied a prior awareness of the problem, the question could be asked why they had taken no action previously to solve the problem. If *Life* magazine could express worry that the Negro community did not turn in the snipers in its midst, would it not be proper to worry why the white community never turned in the violent element in its midst?

The riot made clear that if something is not done about the police immediately, the fears of white society will be transformed into reality: whites will be facing a black society that will not only harbor, but welcome and employ snipers. The troops did not instill fear so much as a fighting hatred in the community. Many people, of every age and background, cursed the soldiers. Women spit at armored cars. Five-year-old kids clenched bottles in their hands. If the troops made a violent move, the primitive missiles were loosed at them. People openly talked of the riot turning into a showdown and, while a great many were afraid, few were willing to be pushed around by the troops. All told there were more than 3000 people arrested, injured, or killed; thousands more witnessed these incidents. From this kind of violence, which touches people personally, springs a commitment to fight back. By the end of the weekend many people spoke of a willingness to die.

Jimmy Cannon was one such person. He was the uncle riding with ten-year-old Eddie Moss when the

Guardsmen shot through the car and the young boy's head was ripped open. Jimmy put the car, blood, bulletholes and all, into a private garage as proof of what happened. Then he was beaten on the street-corner by police who found him there. Jimmy learned how to fight during four years in the Marines. "I don't hold any grudges against you," he told a white person who interviewed him. "I'm just for rights, not for violence. This thing is wrong. I've faced a lot of things, but this is bad, and I just don't care anymore. I am to the point where I just don't care."

By Sunday the crisis was nearing a new stage. If the occupation of Friday and Saturday was going to continue, the community would have started to counterattack in a real way. "Why should we quit," one kid wanted to know, "when they got twenty-five of us and only two of them are dead?"

Perhaps some fear of this trend led Governor Hughes to pull the troops out Monday morning. Perhaps he could see what another three days of occupation would bring. Perhaps, on the other hand, he had no choice. The troops were tired, riots were spreading to other cities of the state, a railroad strike was beginning, and there were all those political engagements awaiting a man with large ambitions. It may also be true that the Governor knew the situation all along but knew as well that 90 per cent of New Jersey is white and frightened. In this view, the Governor took a tough line of support for the troops

60

at the beginning so that withdrawal would be politically acceptable to his white constituency later on.

As late as Sunday night a top state police official was concerned that his men would consider him "chicken" if a pullout was discussed openly. Hughes gave another hard-line speech at a 4 A.M. press conference only hours before the troops left the city.

Does it matter what Richard Hughes believed? Whatever it was, the consequences are what matter finally. The average view of Negroes as "criminals" to be suppressed was reinforced throughout the suburbs of New Jersey. The Negro community learned more deeply why they should hate white people. The police remain a protected and privileged conservative political force, the only such force licensed to kill. With all this coming to pass, few people were joyous as the troops went home on Monday.

V

From Riot to Revolution?

THIS COUNTRY is experiencing its fourth year of urban revolt, yet the message from Newark is that America has learned almost nothing since Watts.

Of primary importance is the fact that no national program exists to deal with the social and economic questions black people are raising. Despite exhaustive hearings over the last five years on problems of manpower and unemployment, anti-poverty programs and the urban crisis, there is no apparent commitment from national power centers to do something constructive.

During the height of the rioting in Newark and Detroit, Congress discussed gun-control laws, voted down with chuckles a bill for rat extermination, and President Johnson set up a commission to do more investigating of the crisis. The main emphasis of governmental remedial programs seems likely to be on

ending the riots rather than dealing with the racial
and economic problem. President Johnson made this
clear in his televised July 28 address on the "deeper
questions" about the riots:

> Explanations may be offered, but nothing can ex-
> cuse what [the rioters] have done. There will be
> attempts to interpret the events of the past few
> days, but when violence strikes, then those in
> public responsibility have an immediate and a very
> different job: *not to analyse but to end disorder.*

When it moves past riot-control to discussion of
social programs, Congress is likely to lament the failure of past civil rights, welfare, and anti-poverty programs, rather than focus on the need for new ones.
As with foreign aid, white politicians (and their voters) tend to view aid to Negroes as a form of "char-
ity" to be trimmed wherever possible, or as a means
of eliminating surplus food, or a way to enlarge urban
patronage roles. Negroes more than likely will be instructed to "help themselves."

But unlike the Italians, Irish, and Jews, black
Americans have always faced a shrinking structure of
economic opportunity in which to "help themselves."
If sheer effort were the answer, the black people
who chopped cotton from dawn to sunset would today
be millionaire suburban homeowners. Self-help does
not build housing, hospitals, and schools. The cost of
making cities livable and institutions responsive is
greater than any sum this country has ever been willing to spend on domestic reform. In addition, the very

64

act of spending such money would disrupt much of the status quo. Private interests, from the real estate lobby and the construction unions to the social work profession, would be threatened. Urban political machines would have to make space for black political power. Good intentions tend to collapse when faced with the necessity for massive spending and structural change.

This political bankruptcy leads directly to the use of military force. When citizens have no political way to deal with revolution, they become counter-revolutionary. The race issue becomes defined exclusively as one of maintaining white society. Holding this view forces the white community to adopt the "jungle attitudes" that they fear the Negroes hold. "Go kill them niggers," white crowds shouted to Guardsmen at 7 o'clock Friday morning as they rode into Newark. During the riot, a *New York Times* reporter was stopped at 2:30 A.M. in Mayor Addonizio's west side neighborhood by a pipe-smoking gentleman carrying (illegally) a shotgun. He explained that a protection society was formed in case "they" should come into the neighborhood. Rifle stores in white neighborhoods all over the east coast are selling out. In such way, the society becomes militarized.

A police "takeover" of local government is not necessary to declare war on Negroes. All that is necessary is to instill in the white citizens the idea that only military force stands between them and black savages. The civilians merely turn over the problem to the troops, who define the problem in terms of using arms to maintain the racial status quo. A typical military attitude in the wake of the riots was offered in the July 29th *Times* by the commander of the New York State National Guard, who said that a greater commitment of force might have prevented rioting around the country. He recommended the use of heavy weapons including hand grenades, recoilless rifles and bazookas. He blamed indecisive civilian authority for making National Guard units operate "with one hand behind their backs" in riot areas.

This military orientation means that outright killing of people is condoned where those people cannot accept law and order as defined by the majority. The country is not moved by the deaths of twenty-five Negro "rioters."

News of a Negro's death is received at most as a tragedy, the inevitable result of looting and lawlessness. When a picture appears of a policeman over a fallen victim, the typical reaction is framed in the terms set by the majority: the dead man is a sniper, a looter, a burner, a criminal. If history is any guide, it is a foregone conclusion that no white policeman will be punished for murder in Newark.

Even many white sympathizers with the Negro cause, and Negro leaders themselves, believe that disorder must be stopped so that, in Roy Wilkins' words, "society can proceed." The question they do not ask is: whose society? They say that Negro rioting will create a backlash suppressing the liberties needed to organize for change. But this accurate prediction overlooks the fact that those very civil liberties have meant little protection for civil rights workers and ordinary black people in the South, and nearly as little for people in the ghettoes of the North. The freedoms that middle-class people correctly feel are real to themselves have very little day-to-day meaning in the ghetto, which is more like a concentration camp than an open society for a large number of its residents. But in order to protect these liberties, many civil rights leaders take part in condemning the ghetto to brutal occupation. Even where "excessive force" is deplored, as Roy Wilkins deplored it in Newark, the assumption still remains that there is a "proper" degree of force that should be used to maintain the status quo. Top officials welcome this liberal support, and agree that any "excessive" force is regrettable and will be investigated. Thus most of the society becomes involved in organizing and protecting murder.

However, the use of force can do nothing but create a demand for greater force. The Newark riot shows that troops cannot make a people surrender. The police had several advantages over the community, particularly in firepower and mechanical mobility. Their pent-up racism gave them a certain amount of energy and morale as well. But as events in the riot showed, the troops could not apply their methods to urban conditions. The problem of precision shooting—for example, at a sniper in a building with forty windows and escape routes through rooftop, alley, and doorway—is nearly as difficult in the urban jungle as precision bombing is in Vietnam. There is a lack of safe cover. There is no front line and no rear, no way to cordon an area completely. A block that is quiet when the troops are present can be the scene of an outbreak the moment the troops leave.

At the same time, the morale fueled by racism soon turns into anxiety. Because of racism, the troops are unfamiliar with both the people and structure of the ghetto. Patrol duty after dark becomes a frightening and exhausting experience, especially for men who want to return alive to their families and homes. A psychology of desperation leads to careless and indiscriminate violence toward the community, including reprisal killing, which inflames the people whom the troops were sent to pacify.

The situation thus contains certain built-in advantages for black people. The community is theirs. They know faces, corners, rooms, alleys. They know whom to trust and whom not to trust. They can switch in seconds from a fighting to a passive posture. It is impressive that state and local officials could not get takers for their offer of money and clemency to anyone turning in a sniper.

This is not a time for radical illusions about "revolution." Stagnancy and conservatism are essential facts of ghetto life. It undoubtedly is true that most Negroes desire the comforts and security that white people possess. There is little revolutionary consciousness or commitment to violence *per se* in the ghetto. Most people in the Newark riot were afraid, unorganized, and helpless when directly facing the automatic weapons. But the actions of white America toward the ghetto are showing black people, especially the young, that they must prepare to fight back.

The conditions slowly are being created for an American form of guerrilla warfare based in the slums. The riot represents a signal of this fundamental change.

To the conservative mind the riot is essentially revolution against civilization. To the liberal mind it is an expression of helpless frustration. While the conservative is hostile and the liberal generous toward those who riot, both assume that the riot is a form of lawless, mob behavior. The liberal will turn conservative if polite methods fail to stem disorder. Against these two fundamentally similar concepts, a third one must be asserted, the concept that a riot represents people making history.

The riot is certainly an awkward, even primitive, form of history-making. But if people are barred from using the sophisticated instruments of the established order for their ends, they will find another way. Rocks and bottles are only a beginning, but they cause more attention than all the reports in Washington. To the people involved, the riot is far less lawless and far more representative than the system of arbitrary rules and prescribed channels which they confront every day. The riot is not a beautiful and romantic experience, but neither is the day-to-day slum life from which the riot springs. Riots will not go away if ignored, and will not be cordoned off. They will only disappear when their energy is absorbed into a more decisive and effective form of history-making.

Men are now appearing in the ghettoes who might turn the energy of the riot to a more organized and continuous revolutionary direction. Middle-class Negro intellectuals (especially students) and Negroes of the ghetto are joining forces. They have found channels closed, the rules of the game stacked, and American democracy a system that excludes them. They understand that the institutions of the white community are unreliable in the absence of black community power. They recognize that national civil-rights leaders will not secure the kind of change that is needed. They assume that disobedience, disorder, and even violence must be risked as the only alternative to continuing slavery.

The role of organized violence is now being carefully considered. During a riot, for instance, a conscious guerrilla can participate in pulling police away from the path of people engaged in attacking stores. He can create disorder in new areas the police think are secure. He can carry the torch, if not all the people, to white neighborhoods and downtown business districts. If necessary, he can successfully shoot to kill.

The guerrilla can employ violence effectively dur-

70

ing times of apparent "peace," too. He can attack, in the suburbs or slums, with paint or bullets, symbols of racial oppression. He can get away with it. If he can force the oppressive power to be passive and defensive at the point where it is administered—by the caseworker, landlord, storeowner, or policeman—he can build people's confidence in their ability to demand change. Persistent, accurately-aimed attacks, which need not be on human life to be effective, might disrupt the administration of the ghetto to a crisis point where a new system would have to be considered.

These tactics of disorder will be defined by the authorities as criminal anarchy. But it may be that disruption will create possibilities of meaningful change. This depends on whether the leaders of ghetto struggles can be more successful in building strong organization than they have been so far. Violence can contribute to shattering the status quo, but only politics and organization can transform it. The ghetto still needs the power to decide its destiny on such matters as urban renewal and housing, social services, policing, and taxation. Tenants still need concrete rights against landlords in public and private housing, or a new system of tenant-controlled living conditions. Welfare clients still need a livable income. Consumers still need to control the quality of merchandise and service in the stores where they shop. Citizens still need effective control over those who police their community. Political structures belonging to the community are needed to bargain for, and maintain control over, funds from government or private sources. In order to build a more decent community while resisting racist power, more than violence is required. People need to create self-government. We are at a point where democracy— the idea and practise of people controlling their lives —is a revolutionary issue in the United States.

Appendix:

The Dead and Brutalized

As of this writing there are twenty-four reported
Negro deaths. Additional reports are being investigated. To give an indication of the kind of stories
that private attorneys and other independent observers are checking, here is part of a statement from an
eyewitness:

> I was standing at the corner of——and——. The
> National Guard were shooting up towards a build-
> ing. There was a lady on the first floor in her
> apartment who was screaming. There was someone
> shooting from the roof of an apartment building.
> Three trucks came and about thirty National
> Guard went into the building. I saw them bring
> out the lady who was dead, and a man came out
> carrying a dead baby. They told the man to stop. I
> heard him say, "You've killed my family, and

> you'll have to kill me if you want me to stop" . . .
> When the lady was brought out a crowd gathered
> and they arrested about thirty people including me.
> Those without a bad record, including myself,
> were released at around 6 A.M. My children were
> left alone all night long.

There are rumors in part of the Newark white community where policemen socialize that forty or forty-
five victims would be a more accurate count. This
possibility is indirectly supported by the statement of
a Negro doctor, E. W. Vernon, who assisted in the
care of patients at Martland Medical Center throughout Saturday night, July 15, and who witnessed three
dead bodies—all Negro—brought in between the
hours of 7:30 and 10:30. "At about midnight and
past they were coming in so fast and furious it was
impossible to take an accurate check on what was
going on," Dr. Vernon said. Incidentally, he supported the statements of a number of witnesses, described earlier, when he indicated that he felt that
"a large percentage of the victims were innocently
involved as attested to by the two young Negro
women who were dead on arrival with history having
been given that they were shot through their
windows."

The Dead

What follows is a brief case-by-case reconstruction
of the killings, based on police accounts, eyewitness

stories, and interviews taken by newsmen and other fact-gatherers.

1. ROSE ABRAHAM, forty-five, 42 Blum St., employed as domestic, married, six children. Mrs. Abraham was awakened late Friday night by the sound of shooting, and went outside to look for her kids. A bullet killed Mrs. Abraham as police shot into a crowd running up Blum Street off Springfield Avenue. Mrs. Abraham was not operated on for six hours after her husband brought her to Martland Medical Center. She died twenty-four hours later. Her sixteen-year-old son fell into a state of shock for several days.

2. ELIZABETH ARTIS, sixty-five, 38 Prince St. Died of a heart attack Sunday, July 16, in her house. Mrs. Artis had had a heart condition for the last four years. During the riot she was in a neighborhood where shooting was extremely severe.

3. TEDOCK BELL, twenty-eight, 411 Bergen. Killed by a bullet in the early hours of Friday. Bell was with relatives and friends, observing wreckage of a bar in which he was employed. He told the others not to run if the police started shooting, because they were not doing anything and might be hurt if seen fleeing. Police fired shots up the street; one person says several shots hit Bell. County Medical Examiner reported Bell was killed by a .38-caliber bullet, the kind police use. Bell was married and had four children, worked as a full-time machinist in addition to bartending, and was a former basketball star.

4. LEROY BOYD, thirty-seven, 322 Belmont. There are conflicting accounts of Mr. Boyd's brutal death. His son told the *Washington Post* that he was in the company of his father near the corner of Belmont and Avon on Friday evening. Police were dispersing people on the street, and put Boyd to the wall for frisking as they did many others. They found nothing. The son said a Negro man shot his father at close range while trying to kill a policeman. However, a funeral home director said Boyd had six .38-caliber bullets in his body, and the Essex County Medical Examiner said he died from a blow delivered by a blunt instrument.

5. REBECCA BROWN, twenty-nine, 298 Bergen. Mrs. Brown was killed when police or National Guardsmen fired into her apartment and many other nearby buildings on Saturday evening. She was attempting to snatch up her two-year-old daughter Delano, who was standing near the window. Mrs. Brown was a nurse's aide at Orange Memorial Hospital. Her husband, who is a construction worker, and four children survive her. A police report said that a "possible bayonet wound" was being investigated, and also that sniper fire may have killed Mrs. Brown.

6. MARY HELEN CAMPBELL, thirty-one, 380

Hawthorne. Police claim Mrs. Campbell was killed while sitting in a stationary car which was struck by a fire engine early Friday morning (about 5:30). Others believe Mrs. Campbell may be the woman who was run down by an official—fire or police—car on 17th Avenue about the same time.

7. RUFUS COUNCIL, early 30s, 1 Prince Street. Mr. Council was eating a chicken sandwich in a steak house at Wickliffe and South Orange Avenue Friday evening. Newark plainclothesmen were seen to drive past, stop, shoot Council as he stepped out of the restaurant, then drive on. This may have occurred shortly after Detective Toto was killed.

8. ISAAC HARRISON, seventy-four, Brooklyn resident. Mr. Harrison was walking to a car from his apartment at Scudder Homes Friday evening when witnesses say a police bullet brought him down. His stepson, who is an officer of the Washington Urban League, said: "The police said they were firing at snipers in the upper stories of the building and I asked them why they were firing at ground level."

9. JESSIE MAE JONES, thirty-one, 255 Fairmount. Mrs. Jones was sitting on her porch early Friday morning after a night of shooting all around her neighborhood. Police report that a Negro man, Mr. Eybind Chandler, 33, was throwing rocks at cars passing along the street. A white motorist in a

Cadillac stopped to go after Chandler, and Chandler chased him with a gun. Chandler's shot missed the car and killed Mrs. Jones. Mrs. Jones' two daughters, according to police, positively identified Chandler, who was indicted July 20 on a charge of homicide. Other observers claim that Mrs. Jones was killed by a white man driving a car past her house after bottles had been thrown at his car. Mrs. Jones, who worked at Hilltop Nursing Home, leaves seven children.

10. WILLIAM FURR, thirty-five, 2 Hollywood Avenue, Montclair. Several witnesses, including *Life* reporters, observed Newark police shoot Mr. Furr Saturday afternoon on Avon Avenue midway between Badger and Livingston. Mr. Furr was carrying beer from a store which had been almost completely looted prior to Saturday. Eyewitnesses say two shots hit Mr. Furr and a third seriously wounded Eddie Bass, a small boy, further down the street. Police and troopers then shot in the air and made everyone go in their houses.

11. HATTIE GAINER, fifty-three, 302 Hunterdon Street. On Saturday evening, shortly after shooting many rounds of fire into nearby Hayes Homes, troopers ran into nearby Hunterdon Street and were shooting into houses. Mrs. Gainer was killed in her second floor apartment in the presence of three grandchildren, ranging in age from three up to seven.

Her daughter recalled police saying, "We made a mistake. We're killing innocent people," while Mrs. Gainer lay on the floor of her house. Mrs. Gainer had lived in the community for twenty years.

12. RAYMOND GILMER, about twenty, living with wife temporarily at mother's house on Bergen Street. For reasons that are unknown, police were chasing Gilmer by car until he parked his car near Clinton and Jelliff about Monday midnight, and ran across the street toward an alley. The police were seen to pull up and fire shots striking Gilmer in the back, then go through his car, where witnesses say they found nothing. However, police claimed Gilmer shot at them, was found with a .38 and knife in hand, stolen clothes and binoculars in car. Married, four kids, employed at State Produce loading potato sacks. Had juvenile record.

13. RAYMOND HAWK, twenty-four, 103 Spruce. Killed by troopers or police in the area of Dayton Street and Frelinghuysen Avenue late Saturday night. Hawk was by himself in the deserted street when police drove by firing down alley at supposed looters. Shot dead in the street as he was trying to get to his car.

14. OSCAR (CURTIS) HILL, fifty, 497 Belmont. Mr. Hill worked at Spring Mountain Tavern on Belmont and Springfield, was a member of the American

Legion and Bartenders Union. He was last seen alive when he left work, wearing his American Legion jacket, about 5 P.M. on Friday the 14th. His body was identified exactly one week later in the morgue by his wife, from whom he had been separated for some time.

15. ROBERT LEE MARTIN, twenty-two, 241 West Market. He went out with his brother-in-law early Friday evening to see what was going on around the corner of Mercer and Springfield. A while later, police began firing up the street. Martin thought they were firing in the air. Then he was hit in the face. He worked nights for a maintenance company. He had come North last year from Greenwood, Mississippi, with his parents and six brothers and sisters. His family reports that money was taken from his body.

16. ALBERT MERSIER, JR., age about twenty, 117 Oliver Street. Police say they shot and killed Mersier late Friday afternoon on Mulberry Street. They reported that he was attempting to load a car with a vacuum cleaner allegedly looted from a nearby burned-out appliance store. When he saw the police he attempted to flee. Police claim that after being ordered to halt, he was shot. Mersier worked as a laborer and lived with his parents and a younger sister.

17. EDDIE MOSS, ten, 240 Rose St. Eddie was

with several members of his family as they were driving to the White Castle for dinner early Friday evening. When his father, who was driving, saw barricades on Elizabeth Avenue near the White Castle, he slowed to a halt. National Guardsmen opened fire. Mr. Moss then drove around the barricades, stopped to let Eddie's uncle jump out to wave down the Guardsmen, then with Eddie's uncle back in the car, drove away to escape further gunfire. When they returned to their neighborhood, the car was riddled with bullets and Eddie was fatally wounded in the head. Police first reported that Eddie was killed by sniper fire, later said an investigation was pending.

18. CORNELIUS MURRAY, twenty-eight, 16 Wainwright. Murray was shot and killed by Newark police about 5 P.M. Friday while standing with relatives near the R & R bar on Jones near Springfield. Police were shooting all over the area. According to the July 24 *Washington Post,* the police who killed Murray "suddenly came over the rooftops spraying the street below with bullets." When Murray first was shot witnesses reported a wound in the back. Later his father said that at the hospital he saw a gash across the top of Murray's head and hole in his head. There were $126 and a ring missing from Murray's body. He worked in a cable company, was married and the father of three.

19. MICHAEL PUGH, twelve, 340 Fifteenth

Ave. About midnight Sunday Michael's mother sent him out with the garbage. The young man that Michael was with said something derogatory to the National Guardsmen who were on the corner, so the soldiers opened fire and killed Michael. He was dead by 1 A.M. Monday. Michael was a sixth grader, and planned to work in the summer anti-poverty program the next day.

20. JAMES RUTLEDGE, nineteen, was inside a boarded-up tavern on Sunday afternoon. Troopers and police broke in. James gave himself up, and was shot point-blank by a trooper. Photographs show that James was hit by about thirty-nine bullets in the chest alone. Evidence indicates not only sadistic killing of James Rutledge, but several incidents of related terror practiced against neighborhood boys.

21. JAMES SANDERS, sixteen, 52 Beacon St. According to police records, James was shot while looting at Springfield Avenue and Jones St. He may have been the youth, about 16, that the Bergen *Record* of July 14 reported killed by two shots in the chest. He may have been the man who was killed by two Newark patrolmen as he ran with liquor bottles through a fence opposite 43 Jones at 4 A.M. (Newark *News,* July 14). James worked as a food distributor at a welfare center. That afternoon he had stopped to see a friend at 298 Bergen, where Rebecca Brown would die two evenings later; he was not seen again. His father, who said James had never been in trouble before, found his son in the City Morgue eight days after he was killed.

22. VICTOR LOUIS SMITH, (?). Police state that Smith had needle marks on his arm when he was found dead in a hallway. The location of the hallway is unclear.

23. ELOISE SPELLMAN, forty-one, 322 Hunterdon, apt. 10E. Mrs. Spellman, a mother of eleven whose husband died several years ago, was shot by police fire as she peeked through her window in Hayes Homes early Saturday evening. Her daughter caught her as she fell, got her brothers and neighbors, then waited forty-five minutes for an ambulance. The family learned late Sunday morning that Mrs. Spellman was dead. Hers was one of many apartments on the side of Hayes Homes facing the 16th Avenue firehouse which were hit by police, troopers and guardsmen as they strafed possible snipers. Mrs. Spellman lived on the tenth floor of a thirteen-story building; bullet marks were visible on Hayes windows from the sixth floor up.

24. RICHARD TALIAFERRO, twenty-five, 100 11th Avenue. Taliaferro was wounded by police while running down South 8th Street about a hundred feet from a liquor store which was looted. Observers say he then was "finished off" by troopers in the street. Taliaferro was due for Army induction July 21.

The Killings of Toto and Moran

The two white persons killed by bullets in the riot were Detective Fred Toto and Fire Captain Michael Moran. Their deaths—Toto at about 6 P.M. Friday and Moran about 10:30 P.M. Saturday—stirred shock and anger in the white community. Both Newark papers carried their photographs and background stories of praise for their contribution: no Negro victims were given such newspaper treatment. It was announced that both were sniper victims.

The assumption that snipers killed these two men undoubtedly triggered a desire for vengeance among many police and firemen. At least one Negro reports having been beaten by police shouting "T-O-T-O." But the evidence in these cases is far too ambiguous to warrant any definite conclusions.

In the case of Toto, the Newark *News* account tells us that he was on duty for twenty-four continuous hours, rested briefly, and was back at work Friday afternoon. Patrolman Paul Buttross was standing next to Toto when, according to Buttross, "we heard some shots from an apartment house across the street. We all ducked low but Fred stood up. I heard a shot, got some flying glass in my face and when I turned around Fred was down." The implication is that Buttross did not actually see who or where the shot that killed Toto came from. Certainly the vast majority of bullets in the air were fired by the troops during the entire period in which Toto was killed; yet it was immediately assumed that snipers were responsible. As a result, it seems fair to assume, the troops opened fire more violently to take revenge. To start out, the July 15 *Daily News* reported that "immediately after Toto was hit, more than 200 national guardsmen, city and state police opened fire on the building where the sniper was believed hiding. The police then rushed the building and seized 25 persons." The New York *Times* described it this way: "guardsmen and policemen, wearing bullet-proof vests and advancing behind armored cars, including an eleven-ton personnel carrier, opened fire on the top floors . . . When they finally secured the building at Mercer and West Street, all the snipers were gone, but some of the hallways were spattered with blood." This attack can only be described as one inspired by the idea of taking massive revenge for a single death. Within a very short time, Rufus Council was shot as he stepped from dinner in a steakhouse, seventy-four-year-old Isaac Harrison was dead as he came to visit his son, and Robert Lee Martin was killed on the streets—all in the immediate geographic vicinity of Toto's slaying. That night, Friday, was to be the bloodiest of the riot.

The case of Fire Captain Moran is even less clear. A few minutes after 10 P.M. Saturday, Moran responded to a fire alarm on Central Avenue a short distance from the station at Central and Ninth. It turned out, according to a signed personal statement of Fire Director John Caulfield, published in the July 17 *Star-Ledger,* that there was no fire visible at the site of the alarm. Caulfield with Moran decided to enter the building. Firemen broke open the second-floor window. Then, Caulfield told the *Star-Ledger,* "the sniper opened fire. *We couldn't see where the bullets were coming from** but we knew from the sound that it was automatic-weapons fire." Caulfield assumes that only snipers use automatic weapons. There then appears a contradiction in two reports of what Caulfield saw. In the *Star-Ledger* he indicates that Moran was standing when hit, and then slumped down behind the truck; at first Caulfield thought the shot struck Moran in the back, "but it was in the lower left side." However, Caulfield is quoted in the Newark *News* of the same date as saying "we heard shots and dropped to the street behind a parked truck." Here Caulfield said he, Moran, two firemen and two Guardsmen were face down behind the fire truck. The Guardsman yelled he was hit, "then Mike yelled that he was hit." In this version Caulfield said that Moran was shot in the abdomen. While lying face down? Caulfield seems sure of this despite the personal account he gave the *Star-Ledger;* he goes on: "We were lying so close it was just a matter of inches who would be killed." Finally, the *News* adds

*Author's italics.

this significant ingredient: *According to Caulfield, it is not certain how many snipers were firing at them or from where the shots were coming."*

There is one further figure in the Moran story: a material witness. At about 10 P.M., approximately twenty-five minutes before the death of Moran, Caulfield related, a car with New York plates drove past Moran's fire station and machine-gunned the front entrance. The driver lost control of the car and smashed into a hydrant by a driveway. Two Negro men fled the car; one was captured one block away by the National Guard, the other was wounded, but apparently not captured, by another Guardsman. Moments later Caulfield arrived and went with Moran to the nearby fire, where Moran was killed. The *News* quoted police as identifying the man captured by the Guardsmen as Howard J. Edwards, 23, of Staten Island; considered as a material witness to the shooting and charged with violating curfew, he was held in lieu of $100,000 bail (the highest charged anyone). The *Star-Ledger* reported also that Edwards was held, and added that "he was arrested in a car not far from the Central Avenue building where Moran was killed. The time of the arrest was shortly after the shooting." The police believe Moran's killer was in the car with Edwards. In one story we are told the two Negro men fled the car, in another story we find that one remained and was arrested. In one story

*Author's italics.

we are told that the unarrested Negro man was wounded, in another that he got from the point of the wreckage to the scene of the supposed fire in time to shoot Moran and a Guardsman, then still could not be found and arrested. In one story we are told the police believe this unknown, wounded Negro to be the killer, while in another story Director Caulfield himself acknowledged that "we couldn't see where the bullets were coming from."

Does this incredible maze of statements seem more believable than the idea that police were firing on themselves and could very well have killed Captain Moran? There were, in fact, some reporters at the scene of the Moran shooting who felt the shots were coming from the police. Certain papers, the *Washington Post* for example, decided to leave unanswered the question of who killed the fire captain. Not so state and local officials. In carrying the myth to 2500 angry firemen at Mike Moran's funeral, they intensified the suspicions and fears of a crucial part of the white community.

Testimony from the Brutalized

Many are alive to tell what happened in the Newark riot. The following stories are adapted from eyewitness accounts collected immediately after the police withdrew. There may be an inaccuracy here, an exaggeration there, but the overall point of these statements is that a broad cross-section of Newark's Negroes have essentially similar feelings about the role of the military during the five days. Because there have been reports of harassment of the individuals cited below, their names have been changed. The sources for the foregoing material are community workers, poverty program officials and persons associated with the American Civil Liberties Union.

• William Anderson was stopped by Guardsmen as he drove home from work early Monday morning. After some discussion over how he was to get home, Mr. Anderson was told, "Black nigger, get in your car and get the hell out of here!" Then police dragged him from his car, saying, "Nigger, what you got in your pocket?" and proceeded to empty his pockets onto the ground. Another said, "You talk about brutality, nigger. We're going to show you what brutality is." After questioning, he was allowed to leave.

• Joseph Adams, fifty-six, was awakened Friday night by loud voices. Watching through his bedroom window, he saw four Newark policemen search five Negro men. The patrolmen informed the men it was after curfew, and one began to beat one of the men with his billy club, while the man begged him to stop. When the beaten man had collapsed, the police ordered his companions to put him in their car and

89

drive off, which they did, in spite of the fact that this incident took place fifty yards from the emergency entrance of Martland Medical Center.

• Around noon on Saturday, Richard Barber, in his mid-twenties, was walking past Foodtown on Broadway with a friend. A white patrolman stopped, handcuffed, and searched the pair, finding a boy-scout knife on Barber, who is a counselor at a camp for ghetto children. The young men were ordered into a squad car. Barber moved a police hat from the seat in order to avoid sitting on it. The officer in the front seat turned, punched Bernard in the thigh, called him a "black son of a bitch," and informed him that he, the policeman, was the boss.

• Jerry Boyd, 52, was watching TV by his window at 11:30 Thursday night. The troops machine-gunned his apartment, breaking five windows and the television. Bleeding from glass cuts, Boyd dropped to the floor.

• Jesus Alvarez was sitting with his family and three friends in his first floor apartment in the Columbus Homes Housing Project at around 9:30 Saturday night, when he heard police order all windows closed. Minutes after obeying this command, and hearing no

90

shots, he and Ramon Rodriguez went into the kitchen for water. Through the window they saw a state trooper standing with a shotgun under a lamppost in the parking lot. Suddenly shotgun pellets struck Alvarez in the chest, and Rodriguez in the neck and shoulder. Both fell to the floor.

• The block on which Leroy Martin and his family live, in an apartment behind their store, is scheduled for urban renewal. Only three families remain on the block. Late Sunday night five rifle bullets passed through the storefront and back into the wall of the bedroom where Martin's wife and daughter were asleep. Martin saw a police car with four white helmeted police pull away from the curb. Half an hour later, Martin watched two state police cars fire into a poolroom, laundromat, tavern, and two vacant buildings on the block.

• Florence Buxton and her brother Andrew Davis were talking with neighbors on her front porch late Friday afternoon, when shooting broke out down the block. She ran into the house. Suddenly Andrew cried out, "My eye, my eye!" and running into the hall Mrs. Buxton saw him leaning against the wall, blood pouring from the side of his head. Andrew Davis has lost the vision in his right eye.

At the same time, down the street, Roger Buxton

was fixing his car. Al Lee, sitting on his stoop next door, watched Roger as he lay on his back with his head under the car. Suddenly Lee saw a state trooper fire at Roger, and heard Roger cry, "I'm hit!" as he clutched his left side, from which blood began to pour immediately.

• Roy Gleason, a newsman, was wearing his press card when he attempted on Saturday morning to take a picture of a trooper searching a suspect. The trooper told him to move on, and when Mr. Gleason answered that he was a member of the press, the trooper responded, "Get moving or I'll take that camera and wrap it around your head!" Shortly afterwards, Gleason watched a white photographer take a picture of a similar searching of a suspect. No remarks were made about moving on.

• Friday night Mrs. Martha Frank saw troopers beat, club, and kick a teen-age boy after asking him, "Where are you going, nigger?" and he replied, "I'm going home."

Minutes later she saw troopers stop a car carrying three Negro men, drag the driver out, ask him where he was going, and immediately hit him on the head with a gun. Another slapped his face, saying, "Don't look at me like that. We ought to kill all of you." The troopers searched the other two men, then beat them with guns until one dropped to the ground. While troopers continued to kick and beat these two, they told the driver, "If you're going to go, go!" When he ran off, troopers chased and caught him, beat him to the ground with guns, handcuffed him and his companions, and put them in a US Army truck.

• Newark Police beat Mr. and Mrs. Richard Lopez on Thursday night as they stood on a street corner. One knocked Lopez to the ground with the barrel of a shotgun, and kicked him in the back, while another kicked his wife in the stomach three times, saying "Kill that nigger bitch!" Mrs. Lopez heard one policeman say, "We had better find a serious charge for her, because we can get in trouble for this." Both were then arrested.

• At midnight, Thursday, David O'Keefe was standing on a crowded street corner. When a policeman driving by told the group to disperse, walked off. Hearing a shot he began to run, and soon realized he had been hit in the left side. When O'Keefe told a policeman he was shot, the policeman knocked him down, kicked him in the ribs, and left him there.

• Robert Baldwin and his white fiancée were stopped on Springfield Avenue Sunday afternoon about 2 P.M. by seven National Guardsmen and two state troopers for what was allegedly an auto search. "Nigger, what are you doing with a white girl? What are you doing with one of our women? Who the fuck do you think you are?"

The troops struck Baldwin several times, then attacked his fiancée while the National Guardsmen called her such things as "Nigger-lover," "white trash," "whore," and "prostitute." Finally, the couple was allowed to proceed home.

• William Brown, a self-employed housepainter, was sitting on the front porch of his home on 15th Street when about fifteen National Guardsmen demanded that everyone evacuate the house. While lying on the front lawn, handcuffed, Brown was beaten with rifle butts and stomped by Guardsmen's boots. Bleeding from head, nose, and arms, Brown was asked where he kept a gun. When he said he didn't have one, they called him "nigger" and repeatedly cursed him.

After the Guardsmen searched the house, $75 was missing from the pocketbook of Brown's elderly aunt, as well as a transistor radio, and cigarettes.

• Lewis Moore, forty-six, a cab-driver for the last fifteen years, was beaten Sunday morning by four Newark policemen whose badges were covered with

94

black tape. "Get out, mother-fucker," he was told, then was beaten around the head with flashlights and rifle butts.

Moore was charged with driving on the wrong side of the street. As a policeman wrote out the tickets, Moore was told: "You son of a bitch, I'll fix you so you don't drive any more cabs . . . Mother-fucker, I saw you taking people down to City Hall the other night."

• Simeol Roberts, a Teamster Union member employed by Red Raven Rubber Co., was awakened Thursday night about 11:30 P.M. by his eighteen-year-old son who pointed out the commotion on the street below.

The two men walked down the hallway but didn't dare to go outside, the two men were attacked by six Newark policemen. Roberts was beaten on the head with a billy club which broke in the process. He was knocked unconscious. Later, he had fourteen stitches.

• Estelle Walker watched National Guardsmen in action near her home Saturday afternoon. In rapid succession, she saw the Guardsmen shoot their guns "in all directions" in reply to a single shot that hit no one, gun down a man carrying a six-pack of beer from a tavern and shoot a woman leaning out a window.

95

• Several days after the riot had ended, Stephen Raymond, a ten-year employee of a large local industrial firm, drove to Newark City Hospital early one morning to take two people for emergency treatment. Raymond was confronted by two shotgun-toting Newark policemen. Raymond told them he was waiting for two patients to be treated. One of the policemen reached through the car window and punched him in the mouth. With that, he was ordered to leave.

• Jonas Ross, Harold Nichols, and Robert Simpson were resting in their home Saturday evening when two state troopers entered the premises. After shooting through the windows, they broke the door down, even though Nichols offered to open it. The state troopers forced the ten occupants of the building's three apartments to lie down on the sidewalk outside. "Let your nose hit the dirt," was the command. Two unloaded and unused guns were impounded.

• Pat Mitchell, a veteran of the Korean conflict and fifteen-year employee of an electronics company, was beaten on the head, stomach, arms, and legs by five Newark policemen inside the Fourth Precinct Thursday evening. Earlier in the day Mitchell had protested police treatment of neighborhood teen-agers. He predicted that the "get-tough" policy would have only "the opposite effect." Mitchell suffered a gash across his forehead requiring five stitches, a possible fractured arm, and innumerable cuts and bruises. No charges were leveled against him.

• John Peters, a seventeen-year-old resident of Columbus Homes, witnessed Newark policemen and state troopers loot cases of liquor from the Colonnade Bar and Grill across the street from his building late Friday night. After shooting into the premises, the police made three trips inside, each time carrying cases out to a yellow emergency truck parked in front. Peters also saw police gun down a Puerto Rican shortly before midnight the same night. He said the Puerto Rican man was unarmed and offered no resistance or provocation.

• Lee Young may lose the full use of his left leg because he was shot by a casually-dressed white motorist near the Pennington Court projects Sunday evening shortly before the curfew. Two bullets extracted from his leg were from a .38-calibre pistol. Young's wound was complicated by a three-and-a-half-hour delay before he was treated. He was questioned by police about the incident during the delay.

• Carlos Nuñez, who lives in a one-family house with

his wife, daughter, and two grandchildren, saw National Guardsmen shoot into his house without warning early Sunday morning. Nuñez quickly took his family to the rear of the house. National Guardsmen entered his house, searched it, found nothing. But all windows of the house facing the street and the roof were hit and broken by bullets.

• Phillip Lloyd, a twenty-one-year-old office maintenance worker, was staying with friends Saturday night on Belmont Avenue. When bottles were thrown from the building where he was, National Guardsmen forced Lloyd and two others into the street below. There he was beaten with blackjacks by two Newark policemen who took $60 from his wallet. At the Fifth Precinct, Lloyd was first told he was being charged with throwing bottles; the charge was changed later to "assault and battery on a National Guardsman."

• Perry Osgood's foot is badly infected because he could not obtain treatment for nearly forty-eight hours while exposed to dirt in the Fifth Precinct and Sussex Avenue armory where he was held. Osgood's foot was cut by glass while running from shotgun-firing Newark policemen Friday evening. "Where do you think you're going, you black bastard?" he was asked after capture.

• Mrs. Rhoda Powers saw police fire into buildings

on both sides of Howard Street Thursday night after someone threw a bottle at them. Nine bullets broke her windows as she dropped to the floor.

• The intersection of Bergen and Hawthorne was crowded with people late Thursday night. Police drove up and down Bergen Street firing their guns. Daniel Lewis, 23, heard a shot, and saw a man lying on the sidewalk bleeding from the shoulder.

• At 3 A.M. Saturday Mrs. Alice Scott and her family were asleep in their apartment. A bullet crashed through the front window, through the living room wall, over Mrs. Scott's bed, and lodged in the wall over her head.

• Friday night Mary Ellen Jones and her daughter Louise were awakened by a bullet exploding through the front window of their third floor apartment. Saturday afternoon the shooting started again and Mrs. Jones and her family hid in the kitchen. Later a fireman told her the state troopers had done the shooting.

• Sally Sinclair was in the kitchen of her Hayes Homes apartment on Saturday afternoon. Bullets began bouncing off the front of the building in an attack that lasted thirty minutes. At half-hour intervals until evening the building was strafed by police and state troopers.

• Susan Wilkes, sitting in her window Saturday evening, saw police shoot into the air from their car as it sped down High Street. Hours later she watched guardsmen fire from tanks and jeeps at nearby rooftops. A tank pulled up in front of her building and fired a cannon-type weapon to the right of her window. She spent the night on the floor.

• Mrs. Alice Jenkins, a welfare mother active in Newark's welfare rights movement was hanging up a shirt in her living room Friday when a bullet ripped through it. Other bullets lodged in the walls and ceiling of her third floor apartment.

• Hubert Morse, forty-five, walked downtown Sunday to buy a newspaper. State troopers stopped and told him to empty his pockets. He put his billfold, $27 in bills, about $2.70 in change and a handkerchief, on the hood of the police car. The troopers were cursing; one of them said "what should happen is they should line up all the niggers and kill them." One officer asked, "Where you going, black boy? When Mr. Morse reached for his bills, the officer put his rifle between the money and Mr. Morse's hand and told him he could put the rest of the items—the small change, the billfold, and the handkerchief— back in his pocket and move on.

• Stanley Ripley, twenty-three, was driving home Sunday night from a visit with his cousin. Troopers and National Guardsmen pulled his car over to the curb. A Guardsman asked him why he was so slow in pulling over, then hit Mr. Ripley in the chest with the butt of his rifle. A trooper then hit him below the belt with the butt of his rifle and asked, "Didn't you hear?" Then he was told to go home.

• Paul Stubbs, thirty-three, arrived home late Sunday night to find his apartment broken into—the windows were smashed, and there were bulletholes in the living room wall. The bedroom closets and bureau drawers had been rifled: a cufflink set with a watch was missing. He phoned the precinct at 8:15 A.M. to report damages and file a complaint. A policeman in the chief's office said, "You're lucky. They're shooting all over Newark, and you are lucky we didn't shoot you. If you have a complaint, come down to headquarters."

• Paula Green could remember no shooting in her West Market Street neighborhood until early Sunday morning when she saw state troopers from her windows, and heard a round of shots. Because of curfew Mrs. Green could not go outside until the next morning: she found her restaurant riddled with bullets. All the other stores along the street with "soul" or "soul brother" signs in the windows were damaged, too.

• Mr. Freddie Collins is afraid to identify the location of his store or residence because he received numerous threatening calls after he was televised accusing police of shooting into his store. Only stores marked "soul brother" on his street were fired into, Mr. Collins said after a Sunday morning survey of the damage.

• Early Sunday morning Paul Sturgeon watched three state troopers break the windows of a Negro-owned business below his apartment. He asked the troopers what they were doing, and was told to "get the fuck back" or be shot.

• Mr. Jonah Gibbons heard the breaking of windows while in the back of his wife's store early Sunday. He saw a Newark policeman outside the store with his rifle raised to break a window. When Mr. Gibbons asked what the policeman was doing, the officer backed away, and shot into the store and the air until a squad car picked him up.

• On Friday afternoon Pat Waters saw several Newark policemen go into the Bilt-Rite Furniture and Appliance Store on Springfield Avenue. A few minutes later they came out with about six portable televisions, put them in a police car, and drove away.

About the Author

TOM HAYDEN was born in Detroit and educated at the University of Michigan, where he participated in student, civil rights, and peace activities. Since 1964 he has been a community organizer in Newark. He is the author of numerous articles on the war on poverty and community organization, as well as co-author of THE OTHER SIDE, with Staughton Lynd, an account of a visit to North Vietnam in 1966.